100+ESSENTIAL GUITAR CHORDS

Wise Publications
London/New York/Paris/Sydney/Copenhagen/Madrid

Exclusive Distributors:
Music Sales Limited
8/9 Frith Street,
London W1D 3JB, England.
Music Sales Pty Limited
120 Rothschild Avenue,
Rosebery, NSW 2018,
Australia.

Order No.AM90135
ISBN 0-7119-3197-6

Compiled by John Moores
Music processed by The Pitts
Cover design by Studio Twenty, London
Computer management by Adam Hay Editorial Design
Printed in the United Kingdom by
Caligraving Limited, Thetford, Norfolk.

Your Guarantee of Quality
As publishers, we strive to produce every book
to the highest commercial standards.
The music has been freshly engraved and the book has been carefully designed
to minimise awkward page turns and to make playing from it a real pleasure.
Throughout, the printing and binding have been planned to ensure a sturdy,
attractive publication which should give years of enjoyment.
If your copy fails to meet our high standards, please inform us
and we will gladly replace it.

Music Sales' complete catalogue lists thousands of titles and is free from your
local music shop, or direct from Music Sales Limited. Please send a
cheque/postal order for £1.50 for postage to: Music Sales Limited,
Newmarket Road, Bury St. Edmunds, Suffolk IP33 3YB.

Also available:
First Chords For Guitar
Order No.AM91072
First Riffs For Guitar
Order No.AM91073
First Scales For Guitar
Order No.AM91074
First Solos For Guitar
Order No.AM91075

Tuning

Accurate tuning of the guitar is essential, and to help you do it easily there is a Guitar Tuning Track on the CD. The correct pitch of each string is sounded long enough for you to tune to it by winding the machine heads up or down. It is always better to tune 'up' to the correct pitch rather than down. Therefore, if you find that the pitch of your string is higher (sharper) than the correct pitch, you should 'wind' down below the correct pitch and then 'tune up' to it.

Relative Tuning

Tuning the guitar to itself without the aid of the CD or pitch pipe.

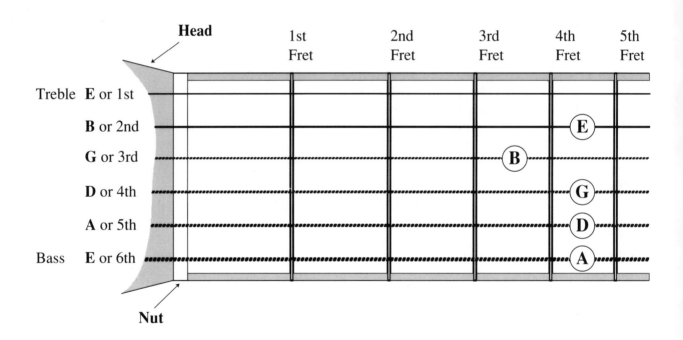

Press down where indicated, one at a time, following the instructions below.

Estimate the pitch of the 6th string as near as possible to **E** or at least a comfortable pitch (not too high, as you might break other strings in tuning up). Then, while checking the various positions on the above diagram, place a finger from your left hand on:

the 5th fret of the E or 6th string and **tune the open A** (or 5th string) to the note Ⓐ

the 5th fret of the A or 5th string and **tune the open D** (or 4th string) to the note Ⓓ

the 5th fret of the D or 4th string and **tune the open G** (or 3rd string) to the note Ⓖ

the 4th fret of the G or 3rd string and **tune the open B** (or 2nd string) to the note Ⓑ

the 5th fret of the B or 2nd string and **tune the open E** (or 1st string) to the note Ⓔ

Chord Boxes

Chord boxes are diagrams of the guitar neck viewed head upwards, face on, as illustrated. The horizontal double line at the top is the nut, the other horizontal lines are the frets. The vertical lines are the strings starting from E (or sixth) on the left to E (or first) on the right.

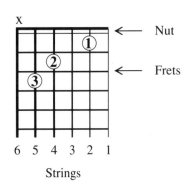

Circles with numbers in them indicate which finger goes where.

Strings marked with an X must not be played. Where no fingering is marked, the open string should be played.

Track 1: Tuning Tones

The C Collection

Track 1:
C major

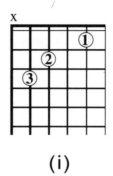

(i) (ii)

Track 2:
Cmaj7

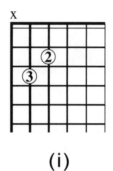

(i) (ii)

Track 3:
C7

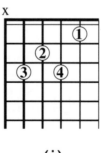

(i) (ii)

Track 4:
Csus4

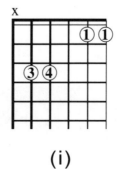

3rd fret

(i) (ii)

Track 5:
C7sus4

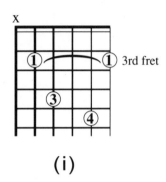 3rd fret

(i)

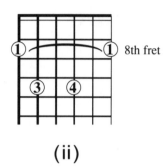 8th fret

(ii)

Track 6:
C minor

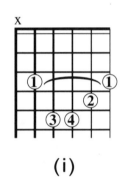

(i)

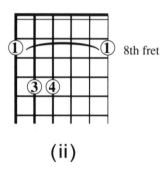 8th fret

(ii)

Track 7:
Cm7

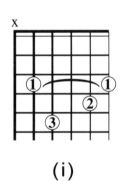

(i)

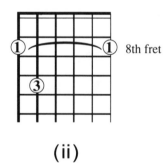 8th fret

(ii)

Track 8:
Cm7♭5

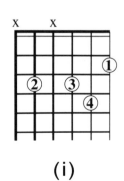

(i)

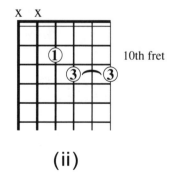 10th fret

(ii)

The C Collection

Track 9:
Cadd⁹

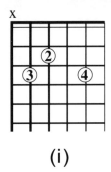

(i)   (ii)   3rd fret

Track 10:
Cdim

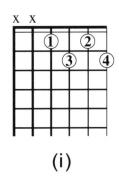

(i)   (ii)

The D Collection

Track 11:
Dmajor

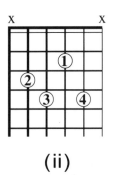

(i)   (ii)   5th fret

Track 12:
Dmaj⁷

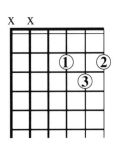

(i)   (ii)   5th fret

Track 13:
D7

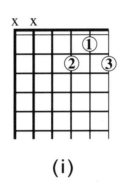

(i)

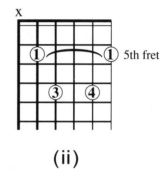

5th fret

(ii)

Track 14:
Dsus4

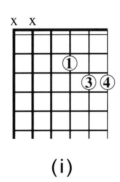

(i)

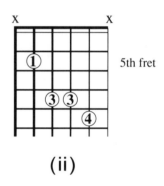

5th fret

(ii)

Track 15:
D7sus4

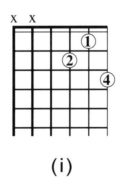

(i)

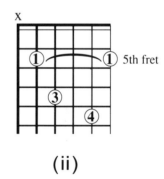

5th fret

(ii)

Track 16:
D minor

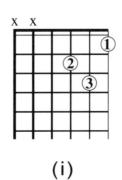

(i)

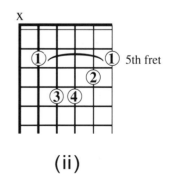

5th fret

(ii)

The D Collection

Track 17:
Dm⁷

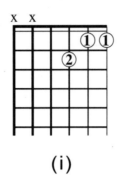

(i)

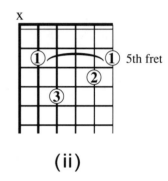

(ii)

Track 18:
Dm⁷♭5

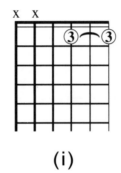

(i)

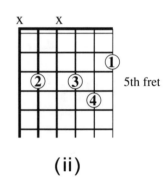

(ii)

Track 19:
Dadd⁹

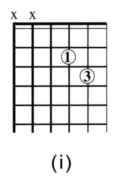

(i)

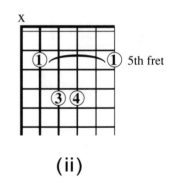

(ii)

Track 20:
Ddim

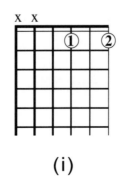

(i)

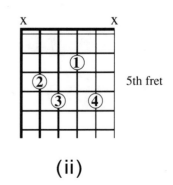

(ii)

10

The E Collection

Track 21: E major

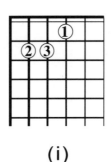

(i)

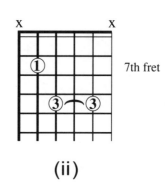

7th fret

(ii)

Track 22: Emaj7

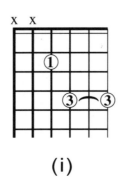

(i)

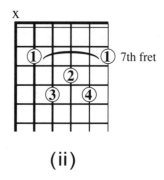

7th fret

(ii)

Track 23: E7

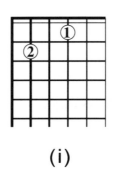

(i)

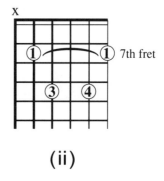

7th fret

(ii)

Track 24: Esus4

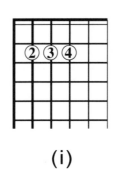

(i)

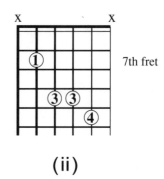

7th fret

(ii)

11

The E Collection

Track 25:
E^{7}sus^4

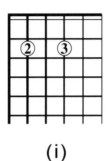

(i)

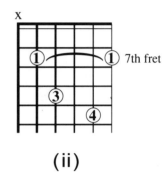

(ii)

Track 26:
E minor

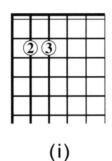

(i)

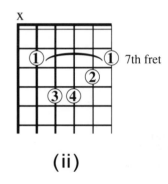

(ii)

Track 27:
Em^7

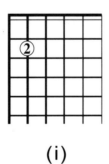

(i)

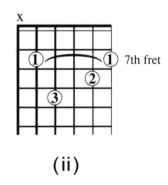

(ii)

Track 28:
Em^{7}b5

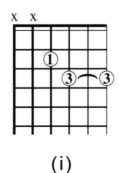

(i)

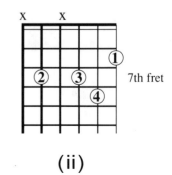

(ii)

Track 29:
Eadd⁹

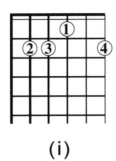

(i)

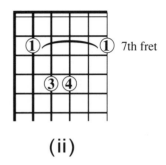

7th fret

(ii)

Track 30:
Edim

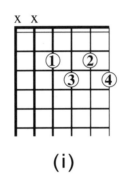

(i)

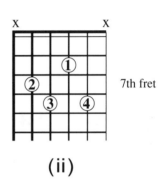

7th fret

(ii)

The F Collection

Track 31:
Fmajor

(i)

8th fret

(ii)

Track 32:
Fmaj⁷

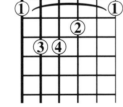

(i)

8th fret

(ii)

13

The F Collection

Track 33:
F7

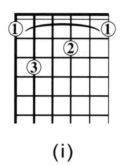

(i)

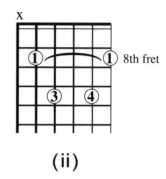

(ii)

Track 34:
Fsus4

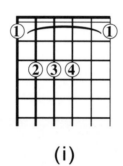

(i)

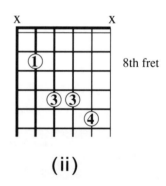

(ii)

Track 35:
F7sus4

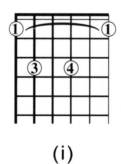

(i)

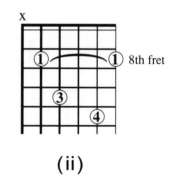

(ii)

Track 36:
F minor

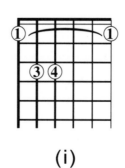

(i)

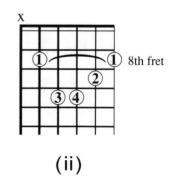

(ii)

14

Track 37:
Fm⁷

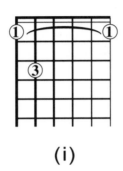

(i)

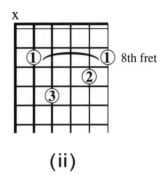

8th fret

(ii)

Track 38:
Fm⁷♭5

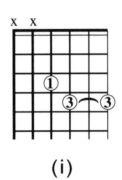

(i)

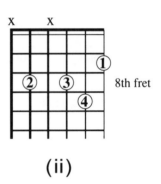

8th fret

(ii)

Track 39:
Fadd⁹

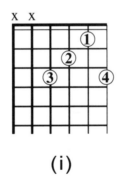

(i)

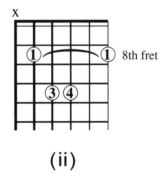

8th fret

(ii)

Track 40:
Fdim

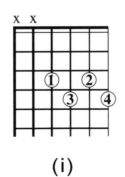

(i)

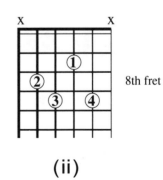

8th fret

(ii)

Track 41:
F#major

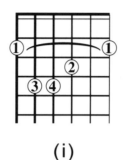

(i)

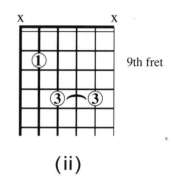

9th fret

(ii)

Track 42:
F#maj7

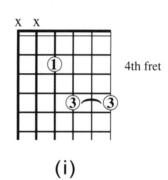

4th fret

(i)

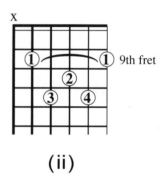

9th fret

(ii)

Track 43:
F#7

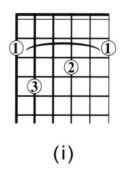

(i)

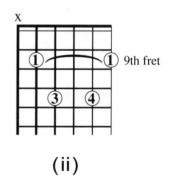

9th fret

(ii)

Track 44:
F#sus4

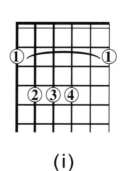

(i)

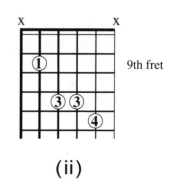

9th fret

(ii)

Track 45:
F#7sus4

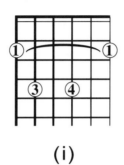

(i)

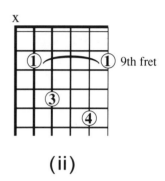

9th fret

(ii)

Track 46:
F#minor

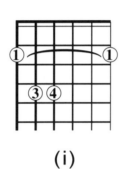

(i)

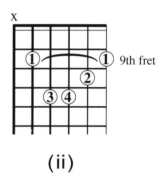

9th fret

(ii)

Track 47:
F#m7

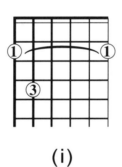

(i)

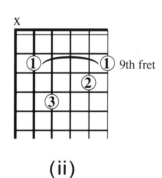

9th fret

(ii)

Track 48:
F#m7b5

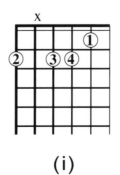

(i)

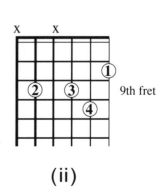

9th fret

(ii)

The F# Collection

Track 49:
F#add9

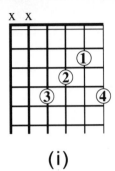

(i)

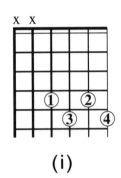

9th fret

(ii)

Track 50:
F#dim

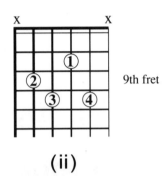

(i)

9th fret

(ii)

The G Collection

Track 51:
G major

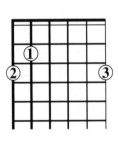

(i)

(ii)

Track 52:
Gmaj7

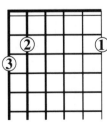

(i)

10th fret

(ii)

Track 53: G⁷

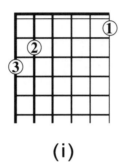

(i)

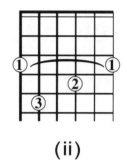

(ii)

Track 54: Gsus⁴

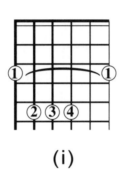

(i)

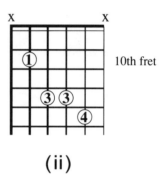

(ii)

Track 55: G⁷sus⁴

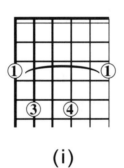

(i)

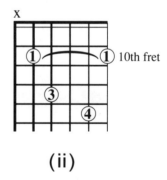

(ii)

Track 56: Gminor

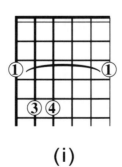

(i)

(ii)

Track 57:
Gmin⁷

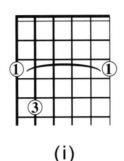

(i)

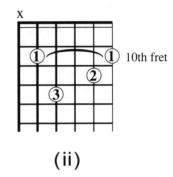

(ii)

Track 58:
Gmin⁷♭5

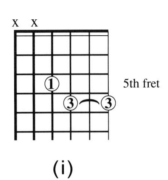

(i)

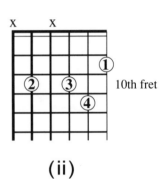

(ii)

Track 59:
Gadd⁹

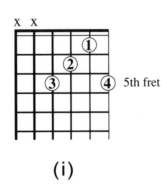

(i)

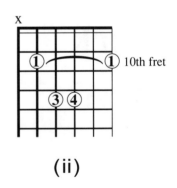

(ii)

Track 60:
Gdim

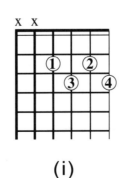

(i)

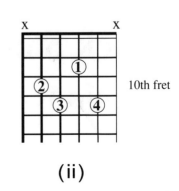

(ii)

Track 61:
Amajor

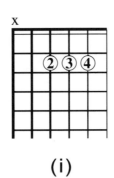

(i)

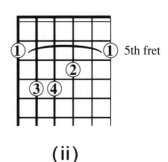

(ii)

Track 62:
Amaj7

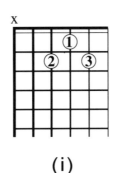

(i)

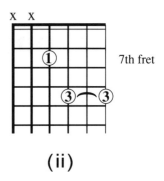

(ii)

Track 63:
A7

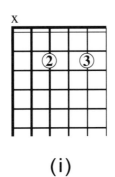

(i)

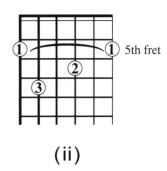

(ii)

Track 64:
Asus4

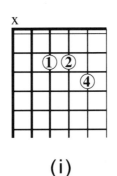

(i)

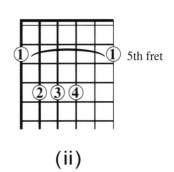

(ii)

Track 65:
A⁷sus⁴

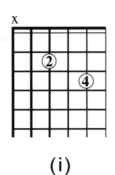

(i)

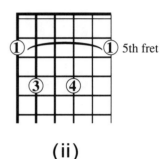

(ii)

Track 66:
A minor

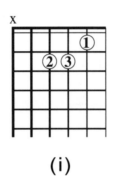

(i)

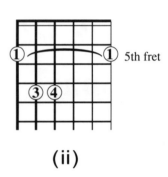

(ii)

Track 67:
Am⁷

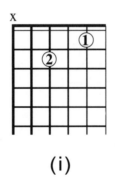

(i)

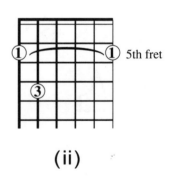

(ii)

Track 68:
Am⁷♭5

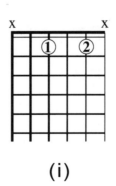

(i)

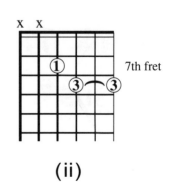

(ii)

Track 69:
A add⁹

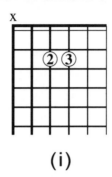

(i)

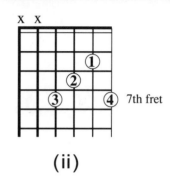

7th fret

(ii)

Track 70:
A dim

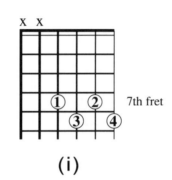

7th fret

(i)

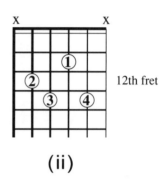

12th fret

(ii)

The B♭ Collection

Track 71:
B♭major

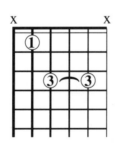

(i)

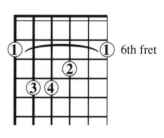

6th fret

(ii)

Track 72:
B♭maj7

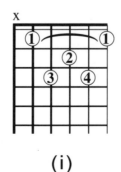

(i)

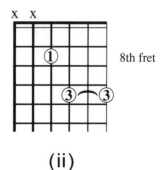

8th fret

(ii)

Track 73:
B♭7

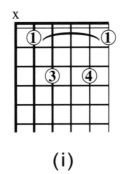

(i)

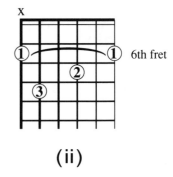

(ii)

Track 74:
B♭sus4

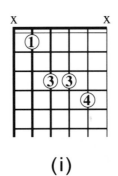

(i)

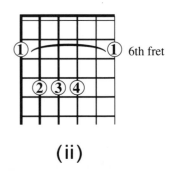

(ii)

Track 75:
B♭7sus4

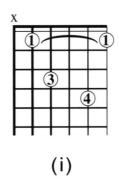

(i)

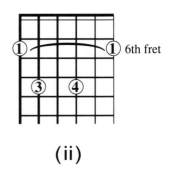

(ii)

Track 76:
B♭minor

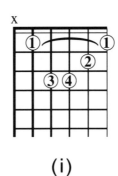

(i)

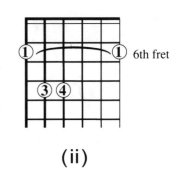

(ii)

Track 77:
B♭m7

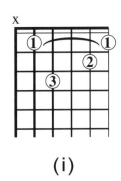

(i)

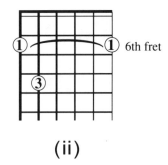

6th fret

(ii)

Track 78:
B♭m7♭5

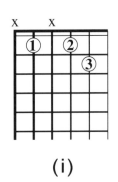

(i)

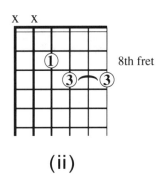

8th fret

(ii)

Track 79:
B♭add9

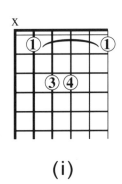

(i)

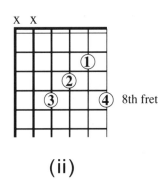

8th fret

(ii)

Track 80:
B♭dim

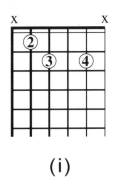

(i)

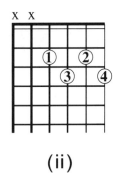

(ii)

Track 81:
B major

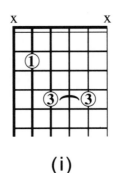

(i)

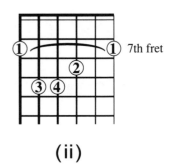

(ii)

Track 82:
Bmaj7

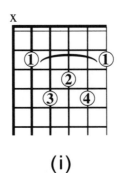

(i)

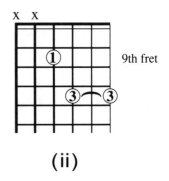

(ii)

Track 83:
B7

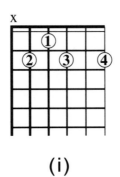

(i)

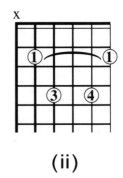

(ii)

Track 84:
Bsus4

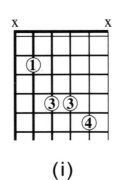

(i)

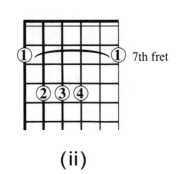

(ii)

Track 85:
B⁷sus⁴

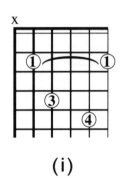

(i)

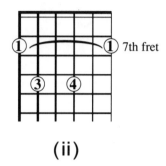

7th fret

(ii)

Track 86:
B minor

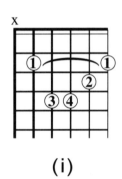

(i)

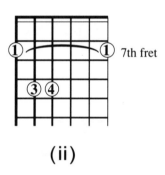

7th fret

(ii)

Track 87:
Bm⁷

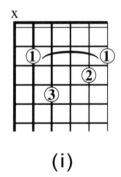

(i)

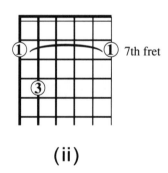

7th fret

(ii)

Track 88:
Bm⁷♭5

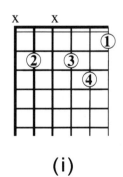

(i)

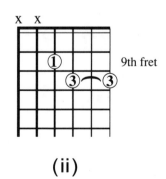

9th fret

(ii)

The B Collection

Track 89:

Badd⁹

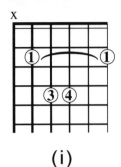

(i)

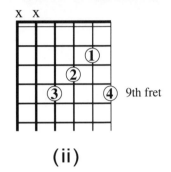

9th fret

(ii)

Track 90:

Bdim

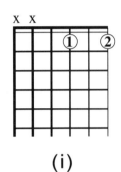

(i)

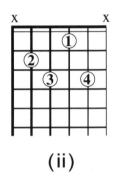

(ii)

Power Chords

Track 91:

Cno3rd

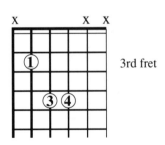

3rd fret

(i)

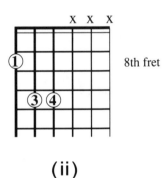

8th fret

(ii)

Track 92:

Dno3rd

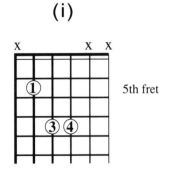

5th fret

(i)

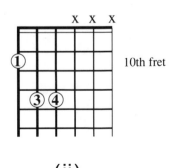

10th fret

(ii)

Track 93:
E no3rd

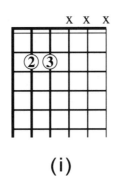

(i)

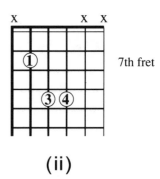

7th fret

(ii)

Track 94:
F no3rd

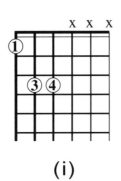

(i)

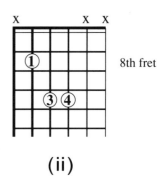

8th fret

(ii)

Track 95:
G no3rd

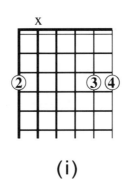

(i)

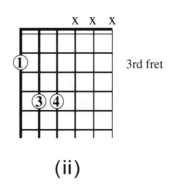

3rd fret

(ii)

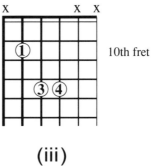

10th fret

(iii)

Power Chords

Track 96:
Ano3rd

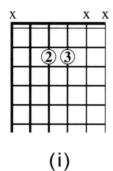

(i)

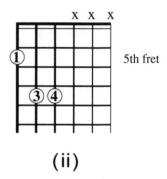

5th fret

(ii)

Track 97:
Bno3rd

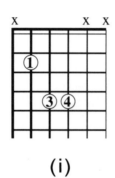

(i)

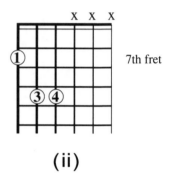

7th fret

(ii)

Now it's time to put it all together!
Listen to track 98, 'Just In Time', and hear how the rhythm guitar is played.
When you are ready, play along with track 99 . Enjoy!!!

Just In Time

$\quad$ = 155

Mike Morendo

4/4 Cno3rd / / / | / / / / | / / / / | B7 / / / ‖

| Em7 / / / | / / / / | Am7 / / / | / / / / |

| Em7 / / / | / / / / | Am7 / / / | / / / / |

| Bm7 / / / C | / / / / | Bm7 / / / | F#m7 / / / |

| Bm7 / / / C | / / / / | Dsus4 / / / | B7 / / / ‖

| Em7 / / / | / / / / | Am7 / / / | / / / / |

| Em7 / / / | / / / / | Am7 / / / | / / / / |

| Bm7 / / / C | / / / / | Bm7 / / / | F#m7 / / / |

| Bm7 / / / C | / / / / | Dsus4 / / / | B7 / / / |

| Em7 / / / | / / / / | Am7 / / / | / / / / |

| Em7 / / / | / / / / | Am7 / / / | / / / / ‖

| Cno3rd / / / | / / / / | / / / / | B7 / / / |

| Em7 / / / |

1/01 (39191)

The Beatles

Enya

Phil Collins

Van Morrison

Bob Dylan

Sting

Paul Simon

Tracy Chapman

Eric Clapton

Pink Floyd

New Kids On The Block

Bryan Adams

Tina Turner

Elton John

Bee Gees

Whitney Houston

AC/DC

Bringing you the
words

All the latest in rock and pop. Plus the brightest and best in West End show scores. Music books for every instrument under the sun. And exciting new teach-yourself ideas like "Let's Play Keyboard" - in cassette/book packs, or on video. Available from all good music shops.

and
music

Music Sales' complete catalogue lists thousands of titles and is available free from your local music shop, or direct from Music Sales Limited. Please send a cheque or postal order for £1.50 (for postage) to:

Music Sales Limited
Newmarket Road,
Bury St Edmunds,
Suffolk IP33 3YB

Buddy

Five Guys Named Moe

Les Misérables

West Side Story

Phantom Of The Opera

Show Boat

The Rocky Horror Show

**Bringing you the
world's best music.**